Wikipedia As A Marketing Tool

Mike Wood

I SG

1 4 0598416 4

ISBN: 1522911014
ISBN-13: 978-1522911012

CONTENTS

FOREWORD

Although *Wikipedia* is an open forum that costs absolutely nothing to use, I have turned it into a steady income in a short time. My career on *Wikipedia* started around 2007 when I was one of the many people who volunteered their time to edit the website for free. I became bored with the website until 2011. It was at that time I read a job posting on a freelance website, asking for help editing a *Wikipedia* page. I responded and was awarded the project. I returned to *Wikipedia* to find that the guidelines and rules had multiplied to the point that you needed to be a surgeon to make an edit or post an article. I quickly regained my *Wikipedia* expertise and have been editing for pay ever since.

I want to start by making a full disclosure: I am not an employee of the Wikimedia Foundation, the non-profit organization responsible for *Wikipedia* and its numerous sister projects.

Any money I make from editing *Wikipedia* comes from outside sources, most notably the people and the companies who have been chased off by the army of bureaucratic volunteer editors who currently run the site.

I am hated by other *Wikipedia* editors, as I found a way to get paid for something they do for free. That is not my issue; it is theirs. In fact, I am hated so much that someone from the Wikimedia Foundation contacted my previous employer, blocked them from even viewing *Wikipedia*, then told them I was editing *Wikipedia* from work (during my lunch hour, of course).

Yes, I was terminated, which I am sure Jimmy Wales and his goons are happy about.

The retaliation described above happened the day after I published an article in *Business Insider*, documenting how I make money to edit *Wikipedia*. It enraged the Foundation so much that it took it upon itself to retaliate.

This is not the only time it retaliated for paid editing. In fact, I have been featured in numerous publications both in the United States and internationally. An article published in *The Atlantic* in 2015 enraged *Wikipedia* editors so much that someone contacted Elance, a popular freelance website, and reported that I was violating the terms and conditions of the Foundation.

Unfortunately for them, I was not, yet it resulted in a short-term block of my Elance account. I no longer personally edit Wikipedia, as I have a team of editors who do this work on my behalf. The process I use in no way violates the Wikimedia Foundation's terms of use or any other guideline on *Wikipedia*.

That being said, I am sure that the Wikimedia Foundation will come after me with accusations once this book is published. I will make sure to write an article on my blog documenting that aggression as well.

I put this book together because of the changes that have taken place with *Wikipedia* over the years. It is so out of control that even co-founder Jimmy Wales has no say in the rules and guidelines (he is only one of thousands of voices that have a say in *Wikipedia* guidelines – as do you).

The rules have become so difficult to understand that many people who create *Wikipedia* pages have them deleted on technicalities (formatting, writing style, promotional tone, etc.). I wanted to share my experience with *Wikipedia* so that people can understand how to use the website for what it was intended, an unbiased encyclopedia. The marketing effect comes with the territory, but you always have to keep the underlying goal of *Wikipedia* in mind.

There needs to be an understanding from both sides (*Wikipedia* editors and those who post articles). I believe both can work together as long as editors stop putting up impossible barriers and marketers stop spamming the site.

Use this book for what it is worth. It won't teach you how to get your article posted simply because you want the article posted. It is a guide that will help simplify the complexity of *Wikipedia* so that you can have an easier time of getting your article on the site.

This book is not about shortcuts, but about understanding the rules and guidelines of *Wikipedia*. You most certainly can use *Wikipedia* as a marketing tool, but you must adhere to guidelines while doing so.

You need to use these guidelines to your advantage, as I have over the years. A well written article that conforms to the guidelines will stand the test of time better than any article that is spammed onto the site. Hopefully by the end of this book, you will be able to determine how to get your article posted, assuming that you still want an article (I'll get into that a little later).

DISCLAIMER

The information contained in this book is current as of the date of publication. As *Wikipedia* is an open source community, rules and guidelines change on a daily basis. This book is intended to be a simple guide on where to get started on *Wikipedia* and should not be considered "advice" in any way, shape, or form. The ultimate success or failure of a *Wikipedia* page depends on the notability of the page, as decided by a consensus of *Wikipedia* editors.

Again, I am not an employee of the Wikimedia Foundation, and any actions you take on *Wikipedia* are your own. As such, you will be responsible for any content you introduce on the site.

Good luck and happy editing!

CHAPTER ONE

What Is So Good About *Wikipedia*?

This is a question that many people have asked over the years. It starts with a friend or an employee who says, "We should get a *Wikipedia* page." It is followed by people in the room looking puzzled, as they don't understand why one website would cause someone to suggest putting in so much time and energy. Let's take a look at some statistics, so that you can draw your own conclusions.

First, take a look at the size of *Wikipedia*. The graph below shows how many books there would be if you were to publish all of the articles currently on *Wikipedia*. You can see how high they would stack. This figure is from January 2011 so you can probably add at least a couple more rows to this graph, by now.

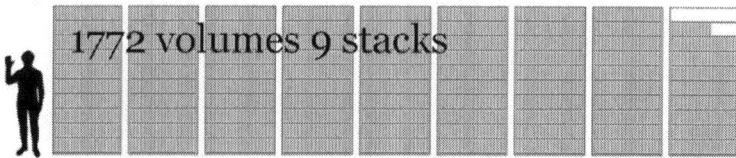

1772 volumes 9 stacks

Size comparison of Wikipedia to actual book volumes. Image courtesy of Wikimedia Commons

Artist Michael Mandiberg created "From Aaaaa! To ZZZap!", a conceptual art piece that some dubbed "print *Wikipedia*." It was displayed at the Denny Gallery in Manhattan in 2015 and symbolized what the entire online encyclopedia would look like, if printed. (Schuessler, 2015)

To give you an idea of how large the project was, it took the website Lulu approximately 24 days to receive the information electronically. Just the volumes listing contributor names covered 36 books. While the piece was only a visual representation for artistic purposes, actual print versions were made available (print on demand) at a cost of $500,000 and included a total of 7,600 volumes and 5.4 million pages. (Schuessler, 2015)

Print Wikipedia by Michael Mandiberg on display in New York City on June 18, 2015.
Image courtesy of Wikimedia Commons.

If you use Alexa to see how your website ranks, both nationally and internationally, you will hit the floor when I reveal how well *Wikipedia* is ranked with Alexa. It has a global rank of 6 and a U.S. rank of 7, with over 2 million websites linking in. (Alexa, n.d.)

Don't worry; I had this book proofed numerous times so you are reading correctly, *6 in the world and 7 in the U.S.* You would need to work a lifetime and get 2 million backlinks to your own website to even come close. *Wikipedia* has done it in a decade and is loved by Google. The following is a comparison of how some of the top websites stand up against Wikipedia.

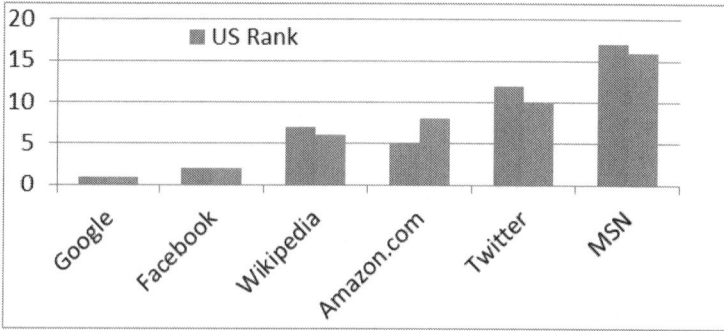

The above data was retrieved from Alexa in March, 2013. This shows how people are using *Wikipedia* MORE than Twitter and Amazon.com. What is surprising is that people are using it more than MSN (people use *Wikipedia* to get their information as opposed to a "search engine"). Wikipedia has become so popular that Google has been accused of stealing traffic from the site with the implementation of the "Google Knowledge Graph." (DeMers, 2015)

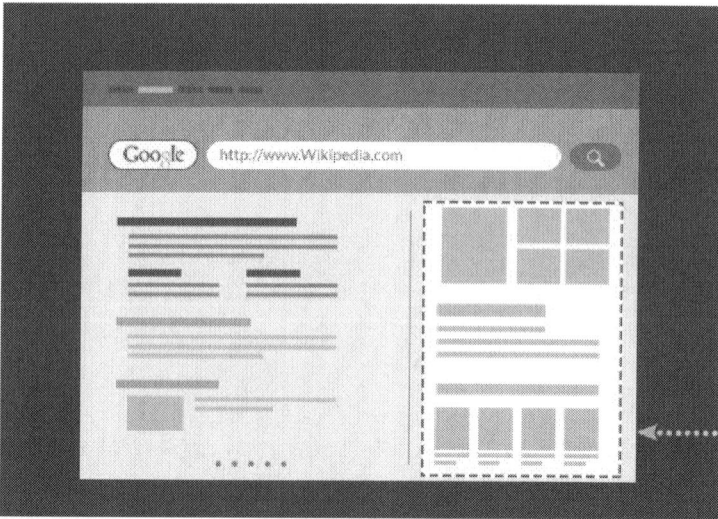

In 2006, Wikipedia was ranked #28 in traffic by Hitwise, but has since moved up the rank to #6. What does this mean for the future of *Wikipedia*?

I am sure that you are already using Twitter and Facebook to promote your business. These social networks rank on either side of *Wikipedia*, so why have you not yet considered a *Wikipedia* page for your company?

People are also using Wikipedia more than similar research sites, such as answers.com and Britannica.com. In fact, *Wikipedia* is used more than answers.com, Britannica.com, encyclopedia.com, and scholarpedia.org combined.

There are also approximately 90 million unique visitors to the site every month in addition to 25,000 edits and 1,500 new articles. (Compete, n.d.) Wikipedia is also said to be responsible for the death of the print encyclopedia. (Olandoff, 2012)

You don't really need to see the fine detail of the chart below. All you need to see is the huge increase on the right-hand side, which denotes the number of articles currently in *Wikipedia* and the increase in the number of articles between 2001 and 2009. It is obvious from the chart that many people are taking to *Wikipedia* in an attempt to get their message across or define who they are.

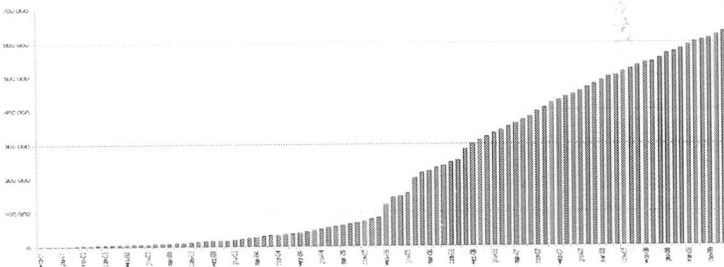

Wikipedia growth through the years. Image courtesy of Wikimedia Commons.

Something else you need to keep in mind, besides the number of articles and visitors, is the relationship between

Wikipedia and Google. Although *Wikipedia* has "no follow" links, Google seems to pay more respect to *Wikipedia* than to any other website. This is largely due to domain authority and domain diversity. (Chant, 2011)

If there is an article in *Wikipedia* focused on the words you are searching for in Google, chances are you will see the Wikipedia entry on the first page of search results and likely in the top two or three results.

If you don't believe me, Google the terms in the table below. I am showing you where the *Wikipedia* page ranked on March 3, 2013. Pay close attention to the last entry, as this is the one you should be concerned with.

Search Term	First Page Rank #
Michael Jackson	#2
Hollywood, California	#1
Pizza Hut	#2
YOUR COMPETITION	?????

These are all archived statistics. Want real time stats from *Wikipedia* itself? Here is a quick list of tools that you can use to view current statistics:

- Overall Stats – This will give you a starting point to all statistics for *Wikipedia*. It includes statistics on ALL Wikimedia projects including *Wikipedia*, Wiki Commons, Wiktionary, and more. (Wikimedia , n.d.) (http://stats.wikimedia.org/)

- Article Popularity – Use this tool to type in the name of an article and you will see how many visitors have viewed that specific article in that last 30, 60, and 90 days. (Grok.se, n.d.) (http://stats.grok.se/)
- Compete – Find the current visitor statistics for *Wikipedia*. (Compete, n.d.) (http://siteanalytics.compete.com/wikipedia.org/?m etric=uv)

Regardless of your opinion of *Wikipedia*, you can't ignore that others are using it as a main source of information. This reason alone is enough to make you stand up and pay attention and have a serious conversation about creating a Wikipedia article about you, your company, or your brand.

CHAPTER TWO

History of the Wiki-Society. Where it was and where it is now.

It always helps to know the history of something before jumping in. *Wikipedia* is no exception.

If you do not know its history, you are less likely to be successful when editing. I bet you have numerous misconceptions about *Wikipedia*; by the end of this book, you will understand differently.

Wikipedia was first launched in 2001. There is a slight controversy over who the official "founder" was, but it is widely accepted that Jimmy Wales is the pioneer. In fact, he is so obsessed with being considered the sole founder, that he has actually edited his own *Wikipedia* article (a "no-no" that I will get into later) to remove the term "co-founder."

He is so obsessed with it, that there is a record of how he has edited his own biography page at least 18 different times. (Mitchell, 2005) He has altered sentences to take credit away from what many believe rightly belongs to "co-founder" Larry Sanger.

Keep Mr. Wales' *Wikipedia* obsession in mind as you read the rest of this book. It will give you an idea of how editors currently act on the site (sort of a Stockholm syndrome).

When *Wikipedia* first came into existence, there were not many editors and new articles were created slowly. Many of those early editors are now considered outcasts to the *Wikipedia* community.

The reliability of *Wikipedia* was often been challenged because of the poor guidelines that were set up in the beginning. Wales himself has stated that some of its entries were a "horrific embarrassment." (The Guardian, 2005) *Wikipedia* is an open community where anyone can edit. You don't even need an account to edit (although it is recommended and preferred by most).

The debate on the reliability of *Wikipedia* continues today, as people rely more and more on its content. Even so, people use it more as something to reference than as as a reference in itself. (Ashman, 2012)

Due to this debate, I put together a free guide of *Wikipedia's* use in academia. The guide shows the best practices for teachers and students and can be found on my website (Legalmorning.com). (Wood, Wikipedia Guide to Notability, n.d.)

Wikipedia is now made up of editors from all walks of life, from those who edit in their parent's basement, all the way through university professors and scientists.

The site's credibility has improved based on the diverse group of editors and the rules and guidelines that have been put into place over the years. Of course, my contention is that the pendulum has swung too far with many of these rules, but they are there and that is why you are reading this. There are even bots that now crawl the site looking for errors in formatting and other errors that could reduce the credibility of an article. (Nasaw, 2012)

The chart below shows the increase in the number of editors since 2001. You can see that, although the number of editors is declining, the number of people editing *Wikipedia* on a regular basis is more than 30,000.

You can also see that, although the number of editors is declining, the number of editors who have a year or more experience is not dropping as fast. This means that the people who are "staying" on *Wikipedia* are those who have been around for a while. So what does this mean?

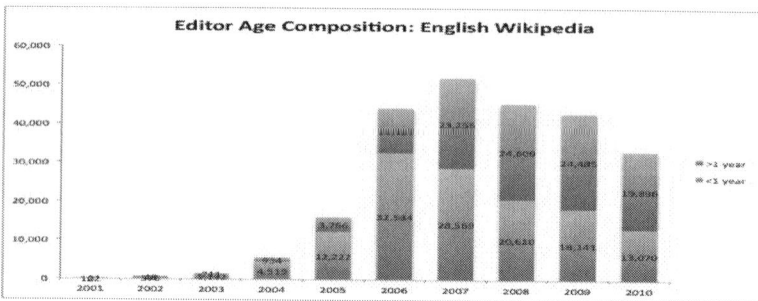

Editor statistics. Image courtesy of Wikimedia Commons.

A post on Theoks.net in 2009 entitled "Reblog: Why I really hate *Wikipedia* administrators" helps explain what is happening with those who are staying on *Wikipedia*.

"Administrators are supposed to be 'helpers'...their function now is to bash users for making accidental edits and to find excuses to block users." (Deathgleaner, 2009)

The post sums up what has happened to *Wikipedia* over the years. The administrators and editors who have been there for a while have turned *Wikipedia* into their own little playground, and they not only make the rules, but also interpret them in a manner most favorable to their own opinions. "Because of administrators, *Wikipedia* has turned into an online totalitarian regime, with administrators at the throne." (Deathgleaner, 2009)

Founder (actually, co-founder) Jimmy Wales has also been quoted with this assessment of the administrators.

"We aren't democratic. Our readers edit the entries, but we're quite snobby. The core community appreciates when someone is knowledgeable, and thinks some people are idiots and shouldn't be writing." – Jimmy Wales (Lewine, 2007)

Wales states "we're quite snobby." By "we", he is referring to the select few who have turned *Wikipedia* into their own community and interpret the policies to keep those they do not want editing from doing so.

What? Did he really just say that? Of course he did; you will see a list of some of his famous "quotes" later in this chapter and get a better understanding of how he operates. *Wikipedia* is an open community where anyone can edit. You don't even need an account to edit (although it is recommended and preferred by most).

In 2007, the *Wikipedia* "inner circle" banned a man by the name of Judd Bagley. Although he had not edited Wikipedia for over a year, the community banned him for writing "about" *Wikipedia*. It was reported that it blocked the edit capability of 1,000 homes (blocking an IP range is common on *Wikipedia*) and retailer Overstock.com in an "attempt to suppress the voice of [Bagley]."

Bagley had written about *Wikipedia* and accused them of using their powers to hijack reality. Bagley was involved as a journalist prior to joining Overstock.com. *Wikipedia* went out of its way to ban Bagley a year after his last edit and after he joined Overstock.com. (Metz, 2007) The story is too long to cover in this book, but you can read the article from The Register. (Metz, 2007) Basically, the *Wikipedia* community wanted him banned so bad that they were willing to block the IP addresses of everyone living in the same town.

Examples of *Wikipedia's* overzealous editing and restrictive policies can be found everywhere. A 2008 article sums things up.

"Something is fundamentally and fatally flawed with *Wikipedia* and it is something which has finally made me give up trying to edit *Wikipedia* articles," says Mark O'Neil. "In other words, *Wikipedia* has no supervisory independent impartial oversight and zealots are going wild with their one-sided view on subjects. They're drunk with the 'editorial power' with which they have been bestowed, they crush all dissent and there's no-one to stop them. The zealots are attempting to influence people with their one-sided view of subjects and if anyone attempts to correct them, well, they're the editors! They're the Thought Police! They'll just change it back again!" (O'Neil, 2008)

Businesses and PR firms are frustrated with *Wikipedia* editing. I am the first to tell my clients that *Wikipedia* is a completely different animal when it comes to writing copy material. PR firms are used to writing masterpieces of press releases and landing page content, but when it comes to *Wikipedia* they simply cannot do it.

It is nearly impossible for PR firms to write for *Wikipedia,* as they are trained to write as persuasively as possible and *Wikipedia* works the opposite way (it is supposed to be non-promotional and neutral). "PR people have long been frustrated by the complexities of the Wikipedia editing process," says a 2012 article in Tech Dirt. "Colleagues tell us they feel rebuffed by what they believe is an arcane system meant to ostracize them whenever they attempt to correct inaccurate or outdated employer or client entries." (Corbett, 2012)

PR people are far from welcome on *Wikipedia.* There are numerous cases of PR firms trying to edit *Wikipedia,* only to be outed and shamed in the media. Jimmy Wales is one of the most vocal about keeping PR professionals from editing *Wikipedia.* As they are a "PR" firm, editors think they are naturally there to push their clients' agenda on the site. This is not always true.

Unfortunately for Jimmy Wales, I am not the only person who feels that he is a menace. On the website Amplicate, 59% state that they hate Jimmy Wales. (Why Do You Hate Jimmy Wales, n.d.) I do not "hate" Jimmy Wales, but he seems to piss a lot of people off. Much of the animosity comes from Jimmy Wales being Jimmy Wales, while the other part comes from people's frustration with editing *Wikipedia.*

Some interesting Jimmy Wales quotes:

- "There's a little bit of monarchy – which is my role in the community." Jimmy Wales speaking at the RSA

Conference in 2013. He also explained the hierarchy of *Wikipedia* from editors to administrators and also likened the powers of administrators to that of an aristocracy. (Thompson, 2013)

- "We have to support our old power users because they build the site." Jimmy Wales speaking with the BBC. He also commented that *Wikipedia* was "too complicated" for many people (a nice way for him to say that his site and his followers are superior – something they will remind you of any chance they get). (Fildes, 2011)

Examples of *Wikipedia* Totalitarianism:

- A PR firm who asked why his client's *Wikipedia* page was deleted received the following answer: "We don't have to explain our editorial decisions to you. If we decide the page goes, then it goes. Get over it. Don't email us again about this matter. You might also want to tell your client that his product sucks." (O'neil, 2008)

- Criticism of subject – Although Wikipedia has a guideline to avoid indirect criticism, editors and administrators often engage in open criticism. (*Wikipedia*, n.d.) During a deletion discussion on a biography of Paul Savramis, the following comments were made: "spectacularly non-notable", "utterly non-notable by every possible WP measurement, "unless he finds Atlantis or levitates (with witnesses) in the next few hours", "Paul Savramis discovers Atlantis while levitating, we still need witnesses though." (*Wikipedia*, n.d.) These are the type of snide comments that editors and admins like to leave in a way to make them feel superior.

These are only two examples of many. I have written numerous articles on my blog at Legalmorning.com that go into deeper detail about many other incidents.

One thing that really has evolved over the years is *Wikipedia's* view on paid editing. Despite there not being a policy prohibiting paid editing, there are terms and conditions that require paid editors to disclose any work they perform on *Wikipedia*. This is to make sure that any edit made by a paid editor can be reviewed for neutrality.

However, the complete opposite happens.

Any editor that discloses their paid affiliations is likely to be chastised and have their edits reversed - not because the editor violated any guidelines, but because *Wikipedia* hates paid editing. Don't believe me? Have a look at the below thread from *Wikipedia* from 2015, describing how editors can watch for paid editing jobs on freelance websites and elsewhere and destroy the resulting articles:

Screenshot of discussion on Wikipedia showing Wikipedia editors stalking people who make money editing Wikipedia.

Jimmy Wales once stated that no one can make money from *Wikipedia*. This is far from true. Gregory Kohs founded MyWikiBiz in 2006. He is the pioneer of professional *Wikipedia* editing. Although a competitor, he has been a mentor to me, helping me understand some of the pitfalls to editing the site.

Paid *Wikipedia* editing has increased over the years, thanks to the bureaucracy of *Wikipedia* and the drop in volunteer editors. Regardless of your feeling towards paid editing, *Wikipedia* editors hate it and will retaliate against it. This is why I have a blanket policy not to show examples of my work to potential clients. Doing so could expose my current clients to rogue editors who assume that I am violating the Foundation's terms of use or Wikipedia's guidelines on editing (neither of which is true). I include a few articles on paid editing at the end of this book. They contain additional examples of how editors like to retaliate against the profession.

To sum it up, what once used to be a level playing field on *Wikipedia* has now turned into a community run by editors and administrators who have been there for years and seem to interpret the policies to fit their positions against any edit they do not like. Although this is the type of conduct that keeps me employed as a paid *Wikipedia* editor, it is the conduct that has turned many off from attempting to edit *Wikipedia* or leaving after only a short time of editing.

Want to know why there are fewer and fewer people volunteering to edit *Wikipedia*? Simply reread this chapter for your answer.

CHAPTER THREE

Should You Have a *Wikipedia* Page?

Now that you know the waters you are dipping your toes into, you need to decide if a *Wikipedia* page is even worth it.

Forget about the complications of creating a page for the moment, and focus on the positives and negatives of having a *Wikipedia* page.

This is an important decision that you need to make. Once you have a *Wikipedia* page, it is unlikely that you can remove it if you decide that you no longer want it.

Benefits of a Wikipedia Page:

I have already discussed some of the benefits of having a *Wikipedia* page. The most obvious is that it will hit the first page of Google. When someone is searching for you, it will be right there and people can, and will, use it to find out what you are all about. Your *Wikipedia* article will link to your website, and it is likely that someone going to *Wikipedia* to find out more about you will ultimately use this link to visit your website. As such, it is a great way to generate more traffic to your site.

Wikipedia pages link to one another. This means that if an article about Mitt Romney talks about the 2012 Presidential Election (which it does), you will find that the words "2012 Presidential Election" will link to the article on the 2012 Presidential Election. Information in that article will also link to Barack Obama, List of Presidents of the United States, Delegates, etc. If you have a *Wikipedia* page, your industry's niche will also be linked to your page.

For instance, if your company is one of the best at manufacturing the XYZ widget, then the XYZ widget page could house a link to your article (either in the "See Also" section or by a keyword talking about your company being one of the best at manufacturing said widget). This gives you exposure, as someone looking at the XYZ widget page could click to your *Wikipedia* page, and ultimately to your website to be converted into a customer (I will also discuss the benefits of leveraging different *Wikipedia* articles to your benefit in Chapter 10).

Brand management is another benefit. I will give you more detail about *Wikipedia* and brand management in the next chapter, but the main idea is that it is beneficial for you to manage your brand before someone else does. By creating a *Wikipedia* page, you are taking control of the content, rather than letting someone else create the page as "they" see it (as their wording might make your company look rather bad).

Hazards of a Wikipedia Page:

"Anyone can make changes, and there is little you can do to keep the public from adding, expanding and telling your story, their way," says Jessica Bowman in a 2007 article on SearchEngineLand.com. Her article talks about how *Wikipedia* is an open source community that anyone can edit and gives advice on how to remove (or dilute) negative information on a *Wikipedia* page. (Bowman, 2007)

Ms. Bowman is correct in her assessment and experience with *Wikipedia*. Once your page is created, it becomes fair game for those who want to edit it. Keep in mind that they must stay within the *Wikipedia* guidelines (I will cover these in greater detail in Chapter 7), but your page will be open to negative content that anyone can add, as long as there is a reliable source to back it up.

CHAPTER FOUR

Wikipedia for Reputation Management

Reputation management takes two main forms. The first is managing negative information about you or your company and attempting to get it pushed to the second page or beyond in the search engines. The other form is brand management, where a company takes control of its brand before anyone engages in negative campaigns against it. Unfortunately, too many companies use the former approach on *Wikipedia* and not enough use the latter.

Managing Negative Content:

When it comes to managing negative information about a company, the worst thing a company can do is create a *Wikipedia* page.

Reputation management often involves creating websites and blogs with well-placed keywords in an attempt to get those pages onto the first page of Google. This helps push any websites with negative content to the second or even third page.

As the majority of searchers never go to the second or third pages, this is a great way to get rid of (actually, "bury") negative content. As people know that *Wikipedia* will ultimately hit the first page, they believe that having a *Wikipedia* page will push the negative content down further. Although true, this is not a good idea.

If a company wants to use *Wikipedia* as a reputation management tool to get rid of negative information, they should think twice. Previously, I talked about the negatives of having a *Wikipedia* page. One of the negatives is that any information that looks bad or is negative about your company can be added to the Wikipedia article, as long as there are sources to support it.

If a company creates a page, it will definitely hit the first page of Google and push the negative content down at least one spot in the search engines. However, someone with a grudge against your company could ultimately add the negative content from the pages that you just pushed to the second or third page.

When added to your *Wikipedia* page, the negative content will rebound in the search results. Plus, your *Wikipedia* article, filled with negative information, will be one of the first hits in Google. In other words, the negative information you tried to bury will be there shinning brightly for all of your potential customers to see. You will essentially erase any reputation management work that you have done and wind up shooting yourself in the foot.

There is one time when I WOULD recommend using a

Wikipedia page for this type of reputation management, but it is very rare and is only a type of damage control.

There are situations when a company or product is so notable that someone will definitely create the *Wikipedia* page soon, such as prescription drugs involved in class action lawsuits. If the page about the drug is not already created, it will be created as soon as the lawsuit story goes national. This is a good time to jump onto *Wikipedia*.

As the page will be created anyway, you may want to get in first and create the page yourself. If you do, you will have a better chance of managing the negative content by writing it from a neutral point of view. Letting someone else write negative content about you can kill your company, but writing negative content about yourself (as long as you keep it neutral and unbiased) can actually provide factual information to those who view the page, as opposed to opinions from those involved as a disgruntled user.

Brand Management:

I recommend reading the OpenForum.com article, *5 Reasons Why You Must Manage Your Personal Brand*, or simply look at the following reasons.

The first question you need to ask yourself is who you want to manage your brand for you. Do you want to be the one to do it, or do you want your customers to do it?

Statistics show that, even though the majority of your customers are more or less satisfied with you, it will be the ones who are not satisfied who will write about you on the Internet. If you want to let them control your online presence, you can put this book down and start making plans to go out of business, as they will drive you into the ground. Managing your brand is something that you want to take control of.

Having a *Wikipedia* page is one way to do that. When people search for your company, they will see your *Wikipedia* article in the top of the search results.

A 2010 article in the *Chronicle* sparked many comments that bring to light how people really use the site. "*Wikipedia* is a great place to start" and "*Wikipedia* is a good source" is all you need to take from the comments as it shows that people will ultimately click on *Wikipedia* prior to your website to learn more about you. Additional comments include "I use *Wikipedia* all the time when I want to learn something quickly", "finding the basic lay of the land is the first step in any research", and "*Wikipedia* has done an amazing job of being the go-to place." (Miller, 2010)

Regardless of your take on *Wikipedia's* credibility, people are using it as their first stop to check out your company.

Another great reason to manage your brand, pointed out by OpenForum, is that your competitors are managing their brands. Transfer this advice to *Wikipedia,* and I can say that your competitors have *Wikipedia* pages.

Do you supply software? If so, you will want to check out your competition on the Wikipedia page for *List of Free Software.*

Are you a book publisher? Then you will want to see your competition at the *list of English-language book publishing companies* on Wikipedia.

Another reason to manage your brand is to make sure that

people see you. Why do you think Nike puts their "swoosh" on the sleeves of shirts worn by NCAA football players? Because they are getting their brand out in front of you.

This is the same reason why you get a little hungry when you see the "golden arches." You want to put your brand out in front of the public and *Wikipedia* is a great way to do it.

CHAPTER FIVE

Leveraging *Wikipedia*

If you have gone through all of the potential positive and negative aspects of having a *Wikipedia* page and still want to create an article, then you should first understand how to leverage *Wikipedia* to your advantage.

Leveraging *Wikipedia* involves you interlinking your article with many others within *Wikipedia* to get the best possible presence that you can. Examples of *Wikipedia* leveraging are as follows:

- **Recording Artists** - For singers and songwriters, it is important to branch out and create additional articles, not just an article about themselves. If they meet notability guidelines, I recommend creating articles about each individual album (and potentially even singles, if they meet notability guidelines). Each article should be linked to and from one another so that visitors to one page are able to click through to the different *Wikipedia* pages related to the artist. This seems like a simple process, but there are several other steps to take: (1) If they sing a song that was used in a video game or a movie, make sure to include that information in the specific *Wikipedia* page for the movie or the video game. (2) Include information about the artist in any list or article about the recording company (e.g., List of ABCXYZ recording artists should include links to artists who are currently signed with ABCXYZ). (3) Include a link to the *Wikipedia* article for any other artist, song, or album they are associated with (e.g., if they collaborated, wrote, produced, etc., then list the artist in the credits for the song's *Wikipedia* article).

- **Companies** – Company pages are pretty simple, as long as they are notable. The work involved can be tedious, depending on the length of the article, but creating the article should not be an issue. To leverage a company article, make sure to include the company in the appropriate lists. For example, a Fortune 500 company's page should be linked from the "list of Fortune 500 companies" page. Another way to leverage one's page is to include information about the company in any other company page they are involved with (e.g., if they were bought out by Microsoft, make sure to include this information with the appropriate reference n the Microsoft page, with a link back to the company's *Wikipedia* article).

- **CEO, Company Directors** – If a person is a CEO or company director, make sure to be linked from the company's *Wikipedia* page. They can also be linked from the college or university where they graduated, in the appropriate article's "notable alumni" section.

While most of the previous examples seem pretty detailed, there are many more ways to leverage *Wikipedia*, including linking appropriate information from your website into an article on *Wikipedia*.

If you have an article posted to your website that is pertinent to a specific term, company, product, person, etc. that has a *Wikipedia* page, add the information to that *Wikipedia* page and use the reference from your website as the source. This also creates a link (no-follow link) from Wikipedia to your website.

I will URGE EXTREME CAUTION here because the content you are linking to must be relevant and useful to the *Wikipedia* community. If your links are being used solely for promotion or are just blatant SPAM, I will be the first one to find them, remove them, and then add your website to the list of blacklisted websites. If you have something valuable to link to another *Wikipedia* article, it is recommended that you hire a professional or ask that the information be added by making an appropriate request on the article talk page.

You have been warned!

CHAPTER SIX

Understanding Notability. The key to every *Wikipedia* page.

Hopefully you are reading this prior to creating your first *Wikipedia* article. After all, a *Wikipedia* article takes preparation and cannot simply be posted without making sure it meets the guidelines. Too often people do not take the time to plan out their path to *Wikipedia* article creation, and wind up with their article deleted. All their hard work is wasted and they face an uphill battle getting the article posted a second time.

The first guideline that is critical for ALL *Wikipedia* articles is "notability." Notability is what makes something (or someone) "good" enough to have their own *Wikipedia* article. You will read many discussions on talk pages and deletion discussions about a topic simply not being "notable" or "doesn't meet notability guidelines." This is a *Wikipedia* editor's way of saying that the topic simply isn't "good" enough to be included in the world's largest encyclopedia.

If you take the time to read this guide, you will understand notability better than most *Wikipedia* editors do. As such, your likelihood of successfully creating a *Wikipedia* article will increase.

Finally, you must keep in mind that I am not the ultimate authority on notability for *Wikipedia*. The *Wikipedia* community of editors as a whole (which includes you) has that say. *Wikipedia* is governed by consensus, so guidelines change based on consensus, as does the interpretation of those guidelines. This guide will help you through the process of understanding notability, but it is ultimately up to you to decide if you feel a topic is notable.

Notability in General

So, what makes something notable?

Well, notability generally comes from references. As a rule of thumb, notability is established when the topic has **"significant coverage"** in **"reliable sources"** that are **"independent"** of the topic. This is sometimes referred to as *Wikipedia's* "Golden Rule." (*Wikipedia*, n.d.)

The statement above is all you need to remember. Once you understand what each term means in regards to *Wikipedia*, you will easily be able to tell if a topic is notable enough.

I put this guide together as notability is commonly misunderstood, both by newbie and experienced editors. *Wikipedia's* guidelines on notability are long and difficult to understand. This guide breaks things down into terms that anyone can understand. After all, you just want to create a *Wikipedia* article, not create a flux capacitor (yes, I age myself with the Back to the Future reference).

However, if you are a bookworm and like to read, you can

look up the countless pages of notability guidelines available on *Wikipedia*. Feel free to read them, study them, burn them, or whatever.

Significant Coverage

Significant coverage means that the topic is covered by numerous sources and those sources cover the topic "in-depth."

Here's an example:

Let's assume we are checking for in-depth coverage of the company The Honest Kitchen, an organic dog food supplier. There are plenty of references out there, which means it has received significant coverage. But which ones can actually be used for notability (as they cover the company "in-depth")?

There are two articles that I looked at to demonstrate Wikipedia's definition of in-depth.

The first is a June 15, 2015 article in the Daily Herald. The article name is "Culver's, Pet Supplies Plus host 4th 'Pets-a-Palooza' fundraiser, adoption event." If you look at the image from the article below, you will see that The Honest Kitchen is talked about. However, it is only a mention of their participation. This is referred to as a "brief mention." While it can be used as a reference to show they participated in the event, it cannot be taken into account for notability.

> p.m. Saturday, June 27, at 250 N. Bolingbrook Dr.
>
> Organizers will raise money for local rescue agencies that rely solely on donations to feed, shelter and place hundreds of animals each year in their combined operations. Both Culver's and Pets Supply Plus will donate 10 percent of that day's sales to these local agencies.
>
> The festivities are free and open to the public and will feature Bolingbrook Police K-9 unit demonstrations, a dog obstacle course, arcade games, build-a-pet station and raffles. Face painters and balloon artists will entertain the children while vendors provide samples of pet food, products and treats. In addition, 95.9/The River will broadcast live from the event.
>
> "Pets help fulfill our lives by providing us with companionship and unconditional love," says Culver's owner Jim DiVerde. "Given that one of every four American households owns a pet, our goal is to help support local humane and rescue agencies so they can continue their vital missions."
>
> Participating sponsors include Blue Buffalo, Natural Balance, The Honest Kitchen, Iams, Eukanuba, Fromm, the Village of Bolingbrook, Bolingbrook Police Department and Bolingbrook Chamber of Commerce.

If all the sources you find on The Honest Kitchen are brief mentions such as the above, the company will not meet the definition of "significant coverage" as there is nothing that talks about the company in-depth.

However, let's take a look at the second example:

The next example is an article from Forbes. The article title is "Does Your Dog Eat Organic? Meet The 'Human Grade' Pet Food Startup." This article talks in-depth about organic dogfood, which is what The Honest Kitchen does. There is a good chance this one will talk about the company.

In fact, you can see below that not only does the article mention The Honest Kitchen, the majority of the article is a feature about the company itself. It details who it is and what it does, and lays out some of the company's history.

This is the type of article that shows notability. Now, there is no set number of articles needed to show notability. As such, I would advise finding as many as you can. Obviously, the more articles you have that talk about the topic in-depth, the more you can show that the topic is notable.

New Posts | Most Popular | Lists | Video | 10 Stocks to Buy Now | Search

7/01/2015 @ 9:44AM | 6,063 views

Does Your Dog Eat Organic? Meet The 'Human Grade' Pet Food Startup

Brian Solomon
Forbes Staff

FOLLOW

Covering all things entrepreneurial.
full bio →

Picture of the company founder is a good sign that the article is going to discuss the topic in-depth

This story appears in the July 20, 2015 issue of Forbes.

+ Comment Now   + Follow Comments

Comment Now

Reliable Sources

The reliability of sources are debated on a daily basis by Wikipedians. Basically, a source is considered reliable if it is from a published source that is trusted. This means that the publication must have editorial control over its content (e.g., fact checkers) and it must be known as being reliable.

As a general rule, simply familiarize yourself with sources used in other articles. Examples of reliable sources include:

The New York Times
The Wall Street Journal
Time Magazine
The USA Today

Topics can also dictate what is considered reliable. For instance, editors generally do not allow references from anything other than peer reviewed medical journals in *Wikipedia* medical articles. This means that although *The New*

York Times may talk about a new breakthrough medical treatment, the *Wikipedia* article about the treatment will generally use only published studies on the treatment, not *The New York Times* article.

If you have a question about a source and whether it is reliable, there is a noticeboard where you can go and pose the question. Simply go there, create a new topic, and ask if a specific link is reliable. You will receive numerous responses from editors who patrol that page on a regular basis. (*Wikipedia*, n.d.)

There is a general checklist that Wikipedia has put together to help you determine if a source is reliable.

So, familiarize yourself with the sources generally used in *Wikipedia*, use the checklist, and consult the noticeboard with any questions about a specific source that you located.

https://en.wikipedia.org/wiki/Wikipedia:Reliable_sources _checklist

Independent of the Topic

Being "independent" can be difficult to understand, especially for those new to *Wikipedia*. However, it is at the core of *Wikipedia* and must be followed in order to maintain its integrity. Simply put, a self-published source is not to be used for notability. There are many times when a self-published source can be used (such as using a company website to source where the headquarters are located), but never for purpose of notability.

Self-published sources can include the following:

Official websites

Social media
Official blog
Press releases

If you want to establish notability with a press release, you are barking up the wrong tree. The article you create will be quickly deleted as the press release is not considered independent of the topic.

As with many other *Wikipedia* guidelines, "independence" can vary depending on the topic. *Wikipedia* provides the following examples:

Examples [edit]

Topic	Independent	Non-independent
Business	Media, government agency	Owner, employees, corporate website, sales brochure, competitor
Person	Media, scholarly book	Person, family members, friends, employer, employees
City	National media, scholarly book	Mayor, local booster clubs

Screenshot of examples of source independence. Taken from source guidelines on Wikipedia.

Here is why it is difficult for newbies to understand. They see self-published sources used all the time in *Wikipedia* which gives a false perception that they are acceptable. **In fact, self-published sources ARE acceptable in *Wikipedia*, but not for establishing notability.**

So, you will find social media profiles, press releases, and company websites cited everywhere on *Wikipedia*, but if they are being used for notability purposes, chances are the topic isn't notable enough for *Wikipedia* and is likely to be deleted.

Additional Notability Guidelines

Now that you understand the "general notability

guidelines," we need to go through the various notability guidelines specific to each topic. Thought we were done didn't you?

These additional guidelines are set up to help editors choose which topics are notable for specific fields. For instance, a different set of notability guidelines apply to "schools" than to "musicians." In fact, most schools equivalent to high school or above are considered defacto notable, as long as you can find a reference to prove it exists. This is a large contrast to guidelines for biographies, which are the most stringent notability guidelines on *Wikipedia*.

I advise you to consult the specific guideline on the topic you are writing about before you attempt to publish your article.

Here is a partial list of additional sub-guidelines on notability for various topics:

- Academics
- Astronomical objects
- Books
- Events
- Films
- Geographic features
- Music
- Numbers
- Organizations and companies
- People
- Sports and athletics
- Web content

CHAPTER SEVEN

Additional Rules You Need to Know

While notability is 90% of the battle, you need to keep some additional guidelines in mind when working with *Wikipedia*. Not all of these guidelines apply in every situation, but knowing them will help you in your editing process.

All of these guidelines are found on *Wikipedia* and I recommend looking through them all (at least briefly) before jumping into any editing.

Conflict of Interest Guidelines

Wikipedia hates editors with conflicts of interest. Of course, most editors have a conflict of interest, as people come to the site to edit topics they are familiar with. With that in mind, make sure you are aware of the *Wikipedia* conflict of interest guidelines.

One of the basic conflict of interest rules for editing is to be transparent by disclosing your interest. It's also suggested (although not required) that you refrain from editing any article you have a conflict of interest with. (*Wikipedia*, n.d.)

Reliable Sources

When it comes to using sources in your *Wikipedia* article, there are stringent guidelines on what sources can be used. The guidelines cover which sources should be used based on the content being cited or type of article being edited.

Wikipedia has guidelines that help you determine what sources are reliable and what sources are not. It also has a reliable source noticeboard where you can ask questions if you are unsure of a particular source. (*Wikipedia*, n.d.)

Assume Good Faith

Although many of the volunteer editors in this bureaucratic regime often ignore this rule, you are still required to follow it. Always assume good faith, which according to the website, is one of the fundamental principles of *Wikipedia*. (*Wikipedia*, n.d.)

No matter what you see on *Wikipedia*, you must always assume that other editors are acting in good faith. As such, you must not initially accuse another editor of violating rules, or accuse anyone of spamming or using multiple accounts, etc. That is, unless you have the evidence to prove it. You must then take up the issue at an appropriate noticeboard.

Long story short...be nice, no matter what.

Manual of Style

Wikipedia has an extensive guide (and sub-guidelines) of the writing style you must use when editing the site. These guidelines include how to title articles, layouts, use of images, and other formatting rules. (*Wikipedia*, n.d.)

Wikipedia is so unique with its Manual of Style that you could take an entire semester to study it and still not know it all.

Deletion Process

Wikipedia has a process by which they rid the website of content that does not belong. This is known as the deletion process and there are specific guidelines regarding how to nominate an article for deletion and under what circumstances an article can be deleted. (Wood, Understanding The *Wikipedia* Deletion Process, 2014)

These guidelines are just the tip of the iceberg, but the ones I listed are some of the most common you will need to know if you plan on editing *Wikipedia* on your own.

CHAPTER EIGHT

Who Will Create Your *Wikipedia* Page? Hope, Pray, or Pay!

There are three ways that you can get a *Wikipedia* page created. The first is to go in and create the article yourself. The next is to hope that someone creates it for you. The final is to hire a professional *Wikipedia* editor to do it for you on your behalf.

Create The Article Yourself

Creating a *Wikipedia* article is not that difficult. That is, if you have quite a bit of experience with using Wikis, understand the thousands of guidelines imposed on contributors, and have the time to write and submit the article. However, with a little bit of learning, being able to create a simple *Wikipedia* article really isn't any more difficult than learning to program your DVR box to record your favorite television shows.

There are many benefits to creating a *Wikipedia* article on your own. First, you will get a sense of accomplishment and have something that you can attribute to creating. Although no one "owns" *Wikipedia* articles that they create, your username will be permanently stamped into the edit history as the article creator. Another benefit is that you do not have to pay anything. When you hire a professional *Wikipedia* editor, the cost can be quite high, depending on the length of the article and how much work will be involved for the editor. Finally, you will have an opportunity to control some of the content (reasonably, within *Wikipedia* guidelines).

A downside to creating a *Wikipedia* article is that it is difficult to write about something that you are close to. In fact, while *Wikipedia* does not forbid creating an article about something you have a close connection with, their guidelines strongly discourage it. Based on recent history and how editors treat the community as their own backyard, any indication that you are close to the subject will cause major issues with the article. For instance, there is a potential for someone to place a "COI tag" at the top of the article as a way of saying "shame on you for writing about yourself."

If you plan on creating the article on your own, you will need to make sure that you are familiar with the conflict of interest guidelines. (*Wikipedia*, n.d.) These are in addition to the guidelines on notability, reliable references and formatting.

Hope the Article is Created

This may seem like a "wing and a prayer" but I will get into a way to speed up this process in the next paragraph. *Wikipedia* articles should be written on notable topics. If the topic that you want written about is notable and receives quite a bit of press, it is likely that someone will decide to create the article for you. Although I am a paid editor, I am addicted to *Wikipedia* and often create articles just for the fun of it. There are hundreds of people who fall into this "hope" category whose prayers have been answered by me just deciding to write about them.

Now, if you want to speed up the process (as there are millions of notable topics that have not been written about in *Wikipedia*, so you are still a small fish in a big pond), you can elicit the help of a little known project in *Wikipedia* called "*Wikipedia* Project Requested Articles." This is where you can list the topic of the article that you would like written about and also leave some information about why you feel it is notable. There are several lists, including sub-categories and sub-categories of the sub-categories. About half a dozen active volunteers create pages from these lists on a regular basis. While adding your article to a list could potentially speed up the creation of your article, the lists are quite lengthy. There are more requests added per day than articles created, so you need to make a good case for your article when you add it to a list.

Hire A Professional

Hiring a professional writer is the quickest way to create a *Wikipedia* page, although I recommend hiring someone with experience rather than just any regular freelance writer. As *Wikipedia* is complicated (as you have already read), you must make sure that you get it right the first time.

CHAPTER NINE

Monitoring Your *Wikipedia* Page

If you have a *Wikipedia* page or plan on creating one, I suggest you also plan on monitoring it. Wikipedia pages change often – some more than others – and it can be damaging to allow inaccurate information to remain unchecked.

People ask me all the time how to "lock" their page so that no one else can edit it. Well, that's not exactly how *Wikipedia* works. Unless the article is the subject of persistent vandalism, it is unlikely it's going to be "locked."

As *Wikipedia* is an open source concept, everyone is allowed to edit. As such, your page is subject to be edited by anyone at any time. All they need to do is follow editing guidelines, and they can easily make a change to the page.

Note that I said "follow the editing guidelines." Just because they can edit *Wikipedia*, doesn't mean that their edits are appropriate or should not be deleted.

By monitoring your *Wikipedia* page, you can be the first to see changes and take action appropriately.

If you do a search for the term "*Wikipedia*" on Google news, you will likely see a news article about how someone's *Wikipedia* page was "vandalized." This often happens to sports figures, when fans express their approval or hatred of a team or an athlete through *Wikipedia*. This is nothing new and will continue as long as *Wikipedia* is operational.

Not all edits on *Wikipedia* are "vandalism", even when they are done intentionally to discredit the article's topic. There are even articles created for the sole purpose of discrediting a subject. This is why monitoring your page is important. In the new world of people hiding behind their computers, *Wikipedia* has become a platform for trolls.

There are two ways to monitor your article. The first is to hire a *Wikipedia* monitoring service (yes, shameless self-promotion, as I run one of these). The other is to do it yourself.

You can sign up for an account on *Wikipedia* and provide your email address (keep in mind that providing your email address could raise privacy concerns – but you must do so if you want to place an article on the list of pages you monitor). Once you do so, you can add pages to your "watch list" and will be notified via email whenever a change takes place to that page. On a side note – make sure you log in to *Wikipedia* every time you receive a change notification. If you fail to do so, you will stop receiving notifications.

CHAPTER TEN

Articles Written About *Wikipedia* Marketing

Over the years I have authored dozens of articles about *Wikipedia* editing. In addition to my personal blog at Legalmorning.com, you can find content I have written posted on websites such as AllBusiness, Social Media Today, Business2Community, Business Insider, and more.

I thought a good way to end this book would be to put together a collection of some of my best work for you to peruse before making up your mind to tackle *Wikipedia* marketing.

How to Do Backlinks in Wikipedia the Right Way

Over the years, Wikipedia has become a minefield for marketers, often causing more trouble than it's worth. However, Wikipedia is still effective and can be used by content marketers to both assist with SEO and contribute to the mission of the world's largest encyclopedia.

Content marketers often misunderstand how backlinks work in Wikipedia. They think that if the topic is relevant, simply adding a link to the "external link" section of a page is good enough. Not so.

Adding a link to Wikipedia is like surgery – if not done correctly it can cause many issues, including having your added domain listed as spam and banned from Wikipedia.

It is so difficult to obtain and maintain a Wikipedia link that I ceased offering this service a long time ago. However, knowing that many marketers are going to do it anyway, I wanted to share some best practices on Wikipedia backlinks. If done correctly, it can still be a great benefit to your SEO.

Going from do-follow to no-follow

First, let's look at how backlinks have changed in Wikipedia over the years. When Wikipedia launched in 2001, backlinks were all "do-follow" – created for SEO purposes. With Google's heavy weighting of Wikipedia and its backlinks, marketers were quick to pick up on the SEO effect.

Wikipedia editors quickly caught on that spam was aplenty. The community took massive steps to help curb spam, including changing links to "no-follow," which have less

SEO effect, and creating a black list to block domains they considered spam. (Cumbrowski, 2007)

Now, even though no-follow backlinks have less effect on SEO than do-follow backlinks, Wikipedia backlinks are still some of the most coveted in the marketing industry. This is because Google gives heavy weight to Wikipedia links despite the fact that they're no-follow.

Identifying where to link

I will share what really works in securing Wikipedia backlinks, based on my professional experience.

- **Do not simply look for citation-needed entries.** Wikipedia automatically searches for and scrutinizes completed citation-needed templates. If the added links do not contribute to the entry's quality, they will be removed and potentially blacklisted.

- **Find entries in dire need of cleanup and expansion.** In these cases, you have a better opportunity to contribute quality content – expanding the knowledge shared on that topic and contributing to Wikipedia's goal of freely sharing knowledge.

To find an article needing more quality information, go to the all-articles-to-be-expanded page. (Wikipedia, n.d.)

More than 1,800 articles fell into this category in one month this fall. Explore more than one month for an endless supply of pages that could benefit from your input.

Knowing the types of links

Now that you know where to find places for your links, let's look at the best-suited types of links:

- **Make sure the links come from a reliable source.** Wikipedia's rules on reliable sources are lengthy. Basically, don't use self-published sources (press releases, etc.) and make sure that the linked website employs fact-checkers to ensure accuracy of content.

- **Check whether Wikipedia already considers the source as reliable.** See if the cited website has its own article. For instance, AdAge has its own Wikipedia page, which increases the likelihood that links from its site will be accepted as a reliable source.

- **See if your cited website has been used as a backlink.** Go to the search box and type in the URL that you want to check. A site that has been used numerous times also increases the chances of it being accepted as a reliable source.

In this screenshot, you can see that AdAge has been used 301 times as a reference in Wikipedia. You also can see the top result is AdAge's own Wikipedia page.

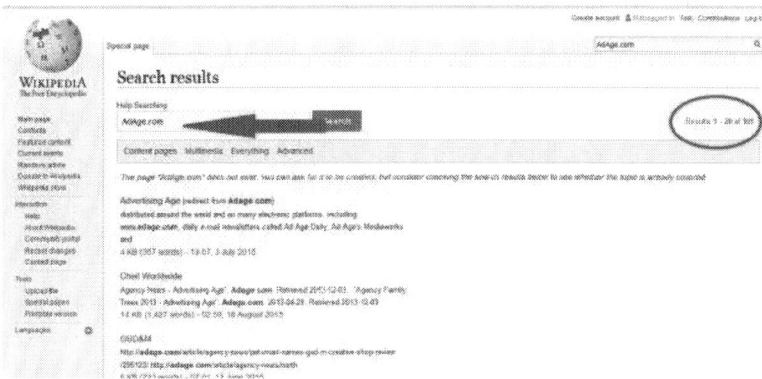

- **Make sure the link is more than a landing page.** A link to a landing page without information to support the content is considered spam by Wikipedia editors.

- **Link directly to the relevant content page.** The link must have content that supports the information you are adding. For instance, if you are adding information about advertising, you cannot simply link to your website's home page as the authoritative source. You must connect to the exact page that supports the content, similar to how you would cite sources in a research paper or industry study.

Putting it together

Now it's time to add the link. To do things correctly, you must contribute to the encyclopedia – adding more links than just the backlink you want to include.

Here is an example of how it works:

Let's say you want to add a link from The Motley Fool to the Big King sandwich article on Wikipedia.

Motley Fool article

http://www.fool.com/investing/general/2014/02/11/could-burger-kings-big-king-be-a-big-mac-killer.aspx

Big King Wikipedia page

https://en.wikipedia.org/wiki/Big_King

The link relates to the advertising of the Big King in 2014 – that section is empty in the entry. Adding the link not only enables you to place the link you want but it also contributes positively to Wikipedia.

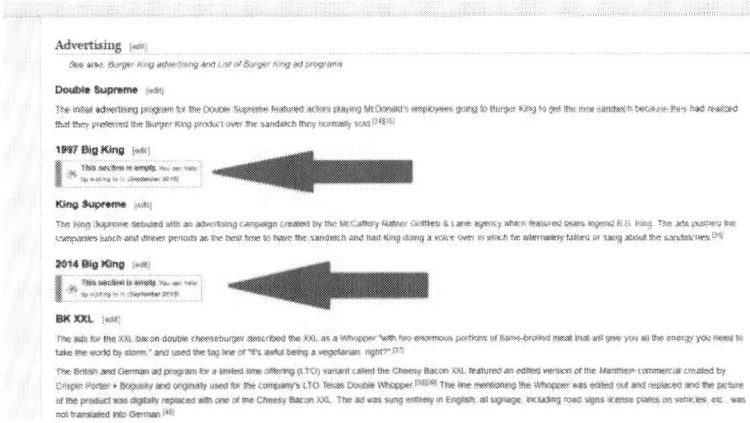

You also have a USA Today citation about advertising of the Big King – although you're not looking to secure a backlink to USA Today, incorporating it adds credibility to the entry.

USA Today article

http://www.usatoday.com/story/money/business/2014/0 2/10/burger-king-mcdonalds-fast-food-big-mac-big-king/5366137/

Now, you must write the content for the entry that is supported by the citations:

"In 2014, Burger King reintroduced the Big King as direct competition to McDonald's Big Mac. (USA Today citation) Part of its advertising campaign was that the beef used on the sandwich was bigger than that of the Big Mac. (The Motley Fool citation)"

By incorporating two credible sources into the added information, you increase the chances that your intended link (The Motley Fool) will survive scrutiny. I also suggest adding even more content to the entry to truly enhance the value of your contribution.

TIP: Follow the proper format to add links. I go in depth into how to do this with a three-step guide for adding citations. (Wood, How to Add a Citation in Wikipedia Like an Expert Wikipedia Writer, 2013) Make sure to know what you are doing – adding a link incorrectly can lead to an editor accusing you of spamming even when you aren't.

In conclusion, I cannot reiterate it enough – do not simply link from Wikipedia for the sake of linking. Make sure to do it correctly and contribute along the way. Introducing content that adds quality to the encyclopedia is likely to help your link last a long time and greatly benefit your SEO efforts. Remember that there is NEVER a guarantee with Wikipedia so any process you employ is not foolproof, just a best practice.

This article originally appeared in Content Marketing Institute.

Why Wikipedia Can Be a Dangerous Reputation Management Tool

Reputation management is something that all companies must be prepared to do in order to protect their brand. There are two main areas of reputation management. The first involves getting out in front of any negative publicity and the other is trying to recover once something negative about your company goes public.

The latter is the most common as many companies are simply not willing to step up and admit a mistake prior to a whistleblower taking the information public. As such, they suffer the consequences and must play catch up in order to protect their reputations.

Through my years as a professional Wikipedia editor, I am often contacted by companies who in some way are looking to use Wikipedia as a reputation management tool.

"My advice to them 99% of the time is to simply walk away and pray that a Wikipedia page about their company is never created."

To help understand the effect that Wikipedia can have on reputation management, it is helpful to understand that one of the most common goals of reputation management is to push any negative content that shows up on the first page of Google results to the second page and beyond. After all, the click thru rate for page two results on Google is less than 2%. (Goodwin, Top Google Result Gets 36.4% of Clicks [Study], 2011)

Logically, you can reduce the effects of negative information about your company by 98% if you can push the negative content to the second page. This is where reputation management companies make their money.

The bulk of revenue for reputation management companies involves pushing negative content to the 2nd page of Google. There are various methods used to do so, but the most common involves article writing.

Well-written articles strategically placed on different websites and optimized with the correct keywords will cause the articles to rise to page one in Google. Once those articles move up to page one, the negative content will be pushed to the bottom and more than likely to the 2nd or 3rd page of Google.

The articles written by reputation management companies contain positive or neutral information about the company they are writing for so that anyone who clicks on the article will not be led to the negative press that previously showed up on the 1st page.

When conducting research on reputation management, companies always come across my favorite statistic about Wikipedia – **Wikipedia Appears on Page 1 of Google for 99% of Searches.** This, according to a study reported by the website Search Engine Watch, shows how much Google loves Wikipedia. (Goodwin, Wikipedia Appears on Page 1 of Google for 99% of Searches [Study], 2012)

Every Wikipedia page that I have ever created has been ranked on page one in less than a week after its creation. Google is said to index new Wikipedia articles every 72 hours; however, many articles that I write wind up on page one in less than 24 hours and some have showed up within an hour. This is a dream for anyone looking to get something positive on page one of Google. Simply create a Wikipedia page about your company and it will rise to the 1st page, pushing down negative content. Hold up! Not so fast!

Using Wikipedia for reputation management can turn out to be a thorn for many and here is why.

Once a Wikipedia page is created, it is unlikely to ever be deleted as long as it meets notability guidelines. This means that once your page is created, it will be there forever. If you are not already familiar with how Wikipedia works, it is an open community of editors where anyone can edit; you don't even need an account. So, even if you have the most gleaming positive article in Wikipedia now, that doesn't mean that what you wrote will stay there forever.

Editors can come along and introduce and/or change information in the article as long as there is a reliable source to back up the edit they performed.

There has always been a debate about the power of Wikipedia backlinks. The links are no-follow links, but seem to have a powerful effect on SEO. With that in mind, sites that are linked from Wikipedia tend to rank higher for the specific page linked.

Now is where your reputation management efforts will be completely erased and here is why......

Once your article is created in Wikipedia, there is a likelihood that someone will come along and introduce the same negative content into the article that you have successfully pushed to the 2nd page of search results. As editors need a reliable source to back up the content they introduce, the same sources that you pushed to page two of Google will likely be used as the supporting source. The effect of these links being in Wikipedia will help bring the negative articles back to page one or at least slightly higher than they already are.

So, in addition to having negative content in your Wikipedia article (the same content you successfully pushed to page two in Google), the Wikipedia article will hit high on page one where everyone can view the negative content. You will also bring back all the negative articles that you pushed out of the 1st page results, basically erasing any reputation management efforts that you previously engaged in. In the end, you will be in worse shape than when you started, which is why Wikipedia should never be used as a reputation management tool.

This article originally appeared in AllBusiness Experts.

Wikipedia Editing – Advice for PR Professionals

The role of PR professionals in editing Wikipedia has been a heated topic over the last couple of years, and remains controversial. On one side, volunteer Wikipedia editors believe that PR professionals are too compromised to write from a neutral or independent point of view. On the other side, public relation folks complain that they are shunned from Wikipedia simply for being in a profession that advocates for its clients.

William Comcowich recently took on the topic for CyberAlert, outlining the history of PR and Wikipedia as well as the role of public relation professionals who edit Wikipedia. (Comcowich, 2015) Comcowich maintained that PR staff should only submit information to editors, not edit content themselves.

This preceded an article in the Huffington Post which featured Wikipedia co-founder Jimmy Wales giving advice to PR professionals. "It's a really bad idea for them to do this because they get caught and it embarrasses their clients," Wales told the Huff Post. (Katz, 2015)

No one knows this better than Sunshine Sachs, a PR firm whose employees were recently exposed for editing Wikipedia pages of clients. (Cieply, 2015) What followed was an onslaught of media about them having a conflict of interest in editing but not addressing the specific edits and whether they were useful for Wikipedia.

It is common for Wikipedia editors to embarrass companies that have a conflict of interest, even if their edits are neutral.

The Wikimedia Foundation's terms of use require anyone receiving compensation for editing on behalf of a client to disclose such conflicts. The purpose is to identify articles for editors to check for neutrality. However, according to PR professionals, the reality is that editors go to the identified articles and place tags on the article in an attempt to shame the company and editor who made the edits.

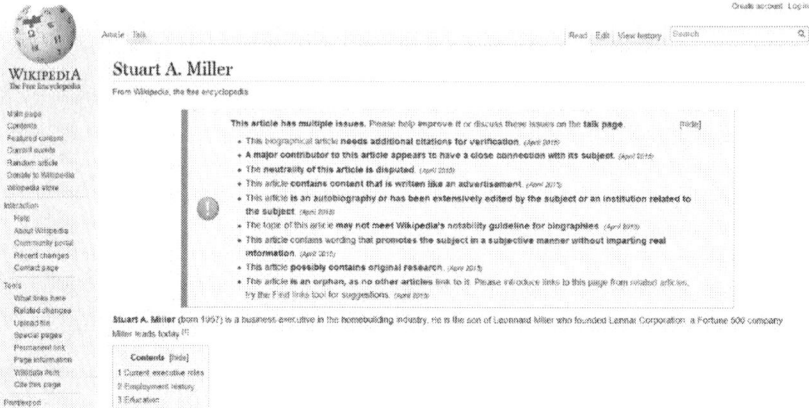

Screen shot of Wikipedia page for Stuart A. Miller showing over-tagging by an overzealous Wikipedia editor.

Editors will likely place tags at the top of articles they believe are written by anyone in the PR profession as this one on Stuart Miller.

Regardless of your position on the subject, the issue is not likely to go away any time soon. Until it is addressed in a manner acceptable to both sides, public relation professionals should adhere to Wikipedia's best practices for editing. While the Wikipedia community has many best practices, here are a few of mine from the viewpoint of a professional Wikipedia editor.

Check Your Writing Style

When writing a Wikipedia article, you should first become familiar with the writing style and article format. Despite having great writing skills, many PR professionals have trouble adapting to Wikipedia's writing style. It's different from standard PR writing and can be difficult to master.

Wikipedia offers many guidelines that will help you, including a manual of style guide that lays out how to title articles, when to use italics, etc.

Examples are your best friend.

When creating a Wikipedia article, I recommend reading a few dozen similar articles before starting your writing. Read older articles, as they better represent the Wikipedia writing style because editors will have polished them over the years.

Pick the best articles as your examples. Do not choose a badly written article and use it as an excuse to incorporate similar information into your article. You will be met by the Wikipedia police who will be quick to point out that "other stuff exists" is no reason to create more of it. (Wikipedia, n.d.)

Notability, Notability, Notability

Notability – the topic importance — is about 75% of the battle in getting content accepted into Wikipedia. The other 25% involves writing style (tone, layout, referencing, etc.). If a topic is not notable, there is really nothing you can do to make it notable. Posting a topic that does not meet specific notability guidelines will cause problems for you and your client when it is deleted. And believe me, it will be deleted.

Be careful when hiring freelance Wikipedia authors. If you're thinking about hiring a professional Wikipedia author, be wary of posting your project on freelance websites. While these are great places to find freelancers, it also attracts attention from the volunteer editor community. Some editors actually stalk these websites looking for paid editors. They will then destroy the article once it goes live on Wikipedia.

If you do elect to use a freelance website, check out the feedback on those who write Wikipedia articles. Once you decide who to hire, post your assignment privately so that only you and the freelancer can view it. This will protect you from the prying eyes of editors looking to redact the work of paid edits.

Keep it short and simple. I always advise people to keep their article as short as possible. Readers are there to obtain basic information, not read your dissertation. As such, it is often better to leave out things such as awards or anything that could seem promotional. If you have a product, simply state what it is and what it does. No one really cares if you made the Inc. 500 list or that your product took five years to develop.

Wikipedia is not a platform for promotion, but having an article about your company or its product in Wikipedia can help with your promotional efforts.

When in doubt, walk away. As a PR professional, your job is to promote your client in the best way possible. A Wikipedia placement about your company or its products is very much a NICE TO HAVE; it is NOT a MUST HAVE for successful public relations or brand promotion. If you can't get a Wikipedia page about your client, there are plenty of other authoritative earned media outlets that accept company and product descriptions.

If your organization has "notability," you play by Wikipedia's rules, you follow Wikipedia's writing style, and you work cooperatively with Wikipedia's volunteer editors, you'll have a pretty good shot at earning a page in Wikipedia.

This article originally appeared in CyberAlert.

Does Your Small Business or Startup Qualify For Wikipedia?

Wikipedia is the 7th most visited website in the world. Since its inception, companies have been using it as a way to establish their brands. Wikipedia can be a great way to promote your business, but it also comes with difficulty. Once of the most difficult things to creating a Wikipedia page is establishing notability.

For companies such as General Motors, Citibank, and Facebook, it is a no brainer that they qualify for a Wikipedia page. The tough part comes when evaluating if a small business or startup qualifies for a Wikipedia page.

Why have a Wikipedia page?

As stated above, Wikipedia is the 7th most visited website in the world. It contains more than 30 million articles, read in over 285 languages, and has 530 million visitors worldwide. In addition, more than 50% of people in the United States use Wikipedia on a monthly basis. This means that even though the accuracy of Wikipedia is disputable, people really don't care. They still use it to determine if they should do business with a company or not.

Wikipedia has an unbelievable search footprint. More than 95% of searches return results from Wikipedia on page one of Google. So much so, that Google incorporates information from Wikipedia into its knowledge graph. (Lasica, Is Google turning from a search engine into a publisher? , 2012)

Having a Wikipedia page can increase your branding power. It will show up on page one of Google and also helps the page rank for your own website.

Do you qualify for a Wikipedia page?

Before you go jumping into creating and posting a Wikipedia page about your company, it is essential to know if you qualify for a page. Wikipedia has tough guidelines for inclusion and failing to meet those guidelines will result in the deletion of your article, and a potential block from being able to recreate the article in the future.

In order to qualify for a page, you must meet Wikipedia notability guidelines. These guidelines basically state that you need to have significant coverage in reliable sources that are independent of the topic.

What types of sources meet the definition of significant, reliable, and independent?

Significant coverage means that there is more than one source that talks about you in depth. Brief mentions do not count. You need articles that are written for and discuss you as the main topic of the article.

Reliable sources can be narrowed down to those who have fact checkers. Using well-known publications such as The New York Times, Business Journals, and other major business publications is acceptable. Using sources such as online forums or social media profiles are not going to help you establish notability.

Independent coverage is simple. You basically need sources that are not self-published. Do not plan on using press releases or your own website to establish notability. If you do, deletion of your article is inevitable.

In addition to the general notability guidelines above, there are individual notability guidelines for specific topics. If you want more in-depth analysis of what constitutes Wikipedia notability, you can download the guide to notability free of charge at Legalmorning.com.

Examples of who qualifies and who doesn't:

To make things a little easier, I evaluated two companies that potentially could qualify for Wikipedia pages. The first is Ubooly and the other is Takhfifan. Both are startups and both have references when you search for them in Google News. And, neither have a Wikipedia page at the time of this posting.

Ubooly is a little stuffed animal with interactive games and playbacks. It incorporates your iPhone or iPod and is intended for children ages four to nine. JD Lasica previously profiled the company for Socialmedia.biz in 2013. (Lasica, Startup turns a smartphone into a smart toy, 2013) Looking at Google, there are plenty of references that come up, including articles in Fast Company, Denver Business Journal, TechCrunch, and more.

It is clear that there is significant coverage, and I will save time by telling you that all of these sources are considered reliable by Wikipedia. The coverage is in-depth as it speaks directly about Ubooly and not just brief mentions (the company name is in the title of each reference). The coverage is also spread about various topics (acquisition, funding, company overview, technology feature) which makes the coverage more than in-depth. Based on what is available, Ubooly would meet guidelines for inclusion in Wikipedia.

Takhfifan is a different story and on the surface looks like it would qualify for a Wikipedia page. However, as of the date of this posting it falls a little short. The company is similar to Groupon, but based in Iran. The company is talked about quite a bit in the press, but very little coverage that is in-depth.

The references that return all include information about Takhfifan, but they are not articles written about the company. Each article is about business in Iran and incorporates information about the company, but are all short of featuring the company. These references would be great for the Wikipedia article about the economy of Iran, but would not qualify to establish the notability of Takhfifan.

Making the decision to create a Wikipedia article:

Once you determine if you qualify for a page, you need to make a decision about actually creating one. While there are many positives to creating a Wikipedia page (previously stated), there are also negatives. Once such negative is that the site is open source and anyone can edit. This means that someone else could potentially introduce information about you on the Wikipedia page you create. There are also conflict of interest guidelines on Wikipedia that discourage you from creating articles about yourself.

Final thoughts on promotion and Wikipedia:

While having a Wikipedia can be exciting, it is not something you have to do to increase your brand presence. I see too many companies addicted to having a Wikipedia that they wind up missing the bigger picture. There are plenty of ways to promote your business outside of Wikipedia. Sometimes the best thing to do is leave it in the hands of the

Wiki gods and hopefully your article will be created once you have enough press to qualify.

This article originally appeared in Socialmedia.biz.

Three Ways Charities Can Make the Most of Wikipedia

According to the website Alexa, Wikipedia is the 7th most visited website in the world. As of 2015, there are more than 325 million people who use Wikipedia. As a website that shows up on the first page of Google, it is no wonder why there is so much traffic to the site. Mike Wood from Legalmorning looks at how charities can make the most of Wikipedia.

So, where does your charity stand with Wikipedia?

Many nonprofits have their own Wikipedia page. As more and more people are using Wikipedia to obtain information, helping your charity expand their Wikipedia presence is a great way to assist with your cause and help people discover more about your nonprofit.

Here are three ways your charity can make the most of Wikipedia.

1. Use Wikipedia to reach more people

One of the first and most obvious ways is to create or edit the article on the nonprofit itself. There are many nonprofits who have Wikipedia pages, but there are many that do not. If your nonprofit doesn't have one, you can create a page yourself.

Another way is to edit the page of a topic related to the organization. For instance, you can edit the page on "multiple sclerosis" to help educate people on the disease. This would help the *Multiple Sclerosis Society* spread the word about what it is and how it affects people.

2. Request funding through the Wikimedia Foundation

The Wikimedia Foundation is the nonprofit arm behind the Wikipedia website. Although it collects donations to advance its own goals, it also provides funding for causes on a case by case basis. Here are the categories that you can request funding for:

Wikimedia Foundation Grantmaking

Travel and Participation Support	Individual Engagement Grants	Project and Event Grants	Annual Plan Grants
Travel funding to participate in mission-aligned events.	Comprehensive support for individual and small team projects focused on online impact.	Expenses related to organizing events and running projects. For individuals, groups and organizations.	Funding the annual budgets and mission objectives of affiliated organizations.

Increasing the quantity, quality, diversity, and reach of free knowledge.

Supporting mission-allied people and organizations around the world.

Screen shot showing the various categories for grants offered by the Wikimedia Foundation.

To request funding for a project, choose which category your project falls under and submit a detailed proposal. (Wikimedia Foundation, n.d.) Funding is not guaranteed, but you have a great shot of obtaining funds if the project not only benefits your organization but also the Wikimedia Foundation and its numerous projects (e.g., Wikipedia, Wikimedia Commons, etc.).

3. Donate images and videos on Wikipedia

Wikimedia Commons is a sister project of Wikipedia that collects media such as images and videos. A great way to help your charity be more visible in search is by donating media to this project. For instance, if your organization fights a particular disease, donating pictures of the diseases' makeup or symptoms as they present in real life is really beneficial to Wikipedia as these images are then used in the articles about the topic. This means that your foundation is contributing to the education of such diseases.

To know which are the best images to donate, simply do a search of Wikipedia for the cause that you support. As an example, let's choose Ebola. A search of Wikipedia finds the article on "Ebola virus disease." Upon looking closer at the article, you can see how people have donated many images that help visualize the disease:

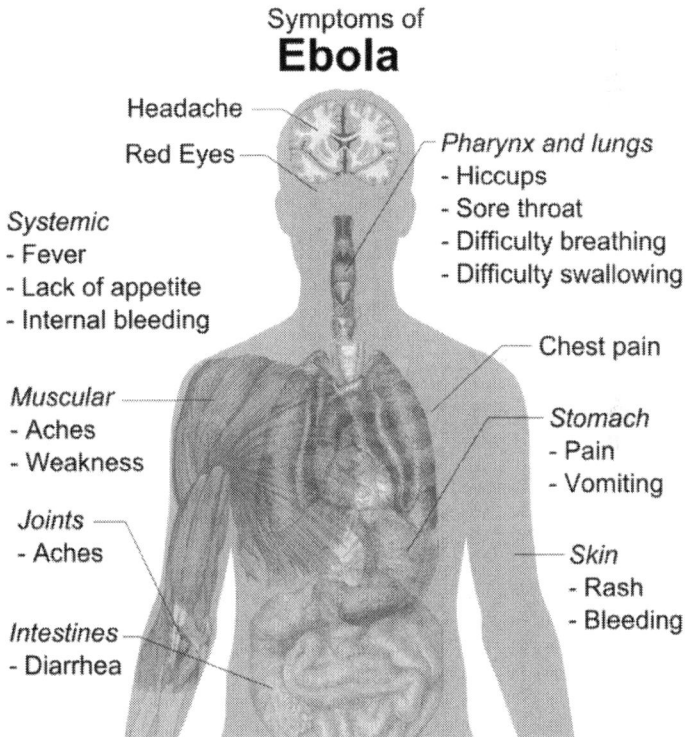

Symptoms of
Ebola

Headache

Red Eyes

Pharynx and lungs
- Hiccups
- Sore throat
- Difficulty breathing
- Difficulty swallowing

Systemic
- Fever
- Lack of appetite
- Internal bleeding

Chest pain

Muscular
- Aches
- Weakness

Stomach
- Pain
- Vomiting

Joints
- Aches

Skin
- Rash
- Bleeding

Intestines
- Diarrhea

Screen shot of examples of source independence. Taken source guidelines on Wikipedia.

If you have images or other media that will help Wikipedia users, then simply upload them to Wikimedia Commons.

Make sure that anything you do on Wikipedia follows their guidelines. Do not spam the site and ensure that any article you create adheres to Wikipedia guidelines – including format, notability, and referencing. If you are unsure of what constitutes notability, you can download the free guide to Wikipedia notability to assist you.

This article originally appeared on the JustGiving blog.

Works Cited

Alexa. (n.d.). *Alexa Website Stats for Wikipedia*. Retrieved March 3, 2013, from Alexa.com: http://www.alexa.com/siteinfo/wikipedia.org

Ashman, M. (2012, March 26). *Students Debate Value of Wikipedia As Reliable Source*. Retrieved February 8, 2013, from Daily Sundial: http://sundial.csun.edu/2012/03/students-debate-value-of-wikipedia-as-reliable-source/

Bowman, J. (2007, June 27). *What To Do When Your Company Wikipedia Page Goes Bad*. Retrieved March 3, 2013, from Search Engine Land: http://searchengineland.com/what-to-do-when-your-company-wikipedia-page-goes-bad-11572

Chant, R. (2011, March 18). *How Small Businesses Can Get a Link from Wikipedia*. Retrieved from Search Engine Watch: http://searchenginewatch.com/sew/opinion/2066183/how-small-businesses-can-get-link-wikipedia

Cieply, M. (2015, June 22). *Wikipedia Pages of Star Clients Altered by P.R. Firm*. Retrieved from The New York Times: http://www.nytimes.com/2015/06/23/business/media/a-pr-firm-alters-the-wiki-reality-of-its-star-clients.html?_r=0

Comcowich, W. (2015, June 30). *Wikipedia Editing Guidelines: The Role of PR*. Retrieved from Cyber Alert: http://www.cyberalert.com/blog/index.php/wikipedia-editing-guidelines-the-role-of-pr/

Compete. (n.d.). *Wikipedia Statistics*. Retrieved March 3, 2013, from Compete: http://siteanalytics.compete.com/wikipedia.org/?metric=uv

Compete. (n.d.). *Wikipedia.org statistics*. Retrieved from Compete: http://siteanalytics.compete.com/wikipedia.org/?metric=uv

Corbett, G. (2012, February 2). *Making The Case For PR Pros Editing Wikipedia*. Retrieved March 3, 2013, from Tech Dirt: http://www.techdirt.com/articles/20120124/12113517528/making-case-pr-pros-editing-wikipedia.shtml

Cumbrowski, C. (2007, January 21). *All Wikipedia Links Are Now NOFOLLOW*. Retrieved from Search Engine Journal: http://www.searchenginejournal.com/all-wikipedia-links-are-now-nofollow/4288/

Deathgleaner. (2009, August 27). *Reblog: Why I Really Hate Wikipedia Administrators*. Retrieved March 3, 2013, from Theoks.net: http://www.theoks.net/blog/2009/08/27/reblog-why-i-really-hate-wikipedia-administrators/

DeMers, J. (2015, September 3). *Is The Google Knowledge Graph Killing Wikipedia?* Retrieved from Forbes: http://www.forbes.com/sites/jaysondemers/2015/09/03/is-the-google-knowledge-graph-killing-wikipedia/

Fildes, J. (2011, January 13). *Jimmy Wales Says Wikipedia Too Complicated For Many*. Retrieved March 3, 2013, from BBC: http://www.bbc.co.uk/news/technology-12171977

Goodwin, D. (2011, April 21). *Top Google Result Gets 36.4% of Clicks [Study]*. Retrieved from Search Engine Watch:

http://searchenginewatch.com/article/2049695/Top-Google-Result-Gets-36.4-of-Clicks-Study

Goodwin, D. (2012, February 13). *Wikipedia Appears on Page 1 of Google for 99% of Searches [Study]*. Retrieved from Search Engine Watch: http://searchenginewatch.com/article/2152194/Wikipedia-Appears-on-Page-1-of-Google-for-99-of-Searches-Study

Grok.se. (n.d.). *Wikipedia article traffic statistics*. Retrieved from Grok.se: http://stats.grok.se/

Katz, E. T. (2015, July 22). *Wikipedia Founder's Message To PR Firms Who Edit Entries*. Retrieved from The Huffington Post: http://www.huffingtonpost.com/entry/wikipedia-founders-message-to-pr-firms-who-edit-entries_55ae919ae4b08f57d5d2b310

Lasica, J. (2012, August 16). *Is Google turning from a search engine into a publisher?*. Retrieved from Socialmedia.biz: http://socialmedia.biz/2012/08/16/is-google-turning-from-a-search-engine-into-a-publisher/

Lasica, J. (2013, March 13). *Startup turns a smartphone into a smart toy*. Retrieved from Socialmedia.biz: http://socialmedia.biz/2013/03/13/startup-turns-a-smartphone-into-a-smart-toy/

Lewine, E. (2007, November 18). *The Encylopedist's Lair*. Retrieved March 3, 2013, from The New York Times: http://www.nytimes.com/2007/11/18/magazine/18wwln-domains-t.html?_r=0

Metz, C. (2007, December 6). *Wikipedia Black Helicopters Circle Utah's Traverse Mountain*. Retrieved March 3, 2013, from The Register:

http://www.theregister.co.uk/2007/12/06/wikipedia_an
d_overstock/

Miller, M. H. (2010, March 16). *Students Use Wikipedia Early and
Often*. Retrieved February 24, 2013, from Chronicle:
http://chronicle.com/blogs/wiredcampus/students-use-
wikipedia-earlyoften/21850

Mitchell, D. (2005, December 24). *Insider Editing At Wikipedia*.
Retrieved February 8, 2013, from New York Times:
http://www.nytimes.com/2005/12/24/technology/24onl
ine.ready.html?_r=0

Nasaw, D. (2012, July 24). *Meet The 'Bots' That Edit Wikipedia*.
Retrieved February 8, 2013, from BBC:
http://www.bbc.co.uk/news/magazine-18892510

Olandoff, D. (2012, March 13). *Wikipedia and the Internet just killed
244-year-old Encyclopaedia Britannica*. Retrieved from The
Next Web:
http://thenextweb.com/media/2012/03/13/wikipedia-
and-the-internet-just-killed-244-year-old-encyclopaedia-
britannica/

O'neil, M. (2008, April 26). *The Wikipedia Thought Police*. Retrieved
March 3, 2013, from Geekss Are Sexy:
http://www.geeksaresexy.net/2008/04/26/the-
wikipedia-thought-police/

Schuessler, J. (2015, July 13). *Print Wikipedia Project Reaches Final
Entry*. Retrieved from The New York Times:
http://artsbeat.blogs.nytimes.com/2015/07/13/print-
wikipedia-project-reaches-final-entry/

The Guardian. (2005, October 23). *Can You Trust Wikipedia?*
Retrieved February 8, 2013, from The Guardian:

http://www.guardian.co.uk/technology/2005/oct/24/co
mment.newmedia

Thompson, L. (2013, February 28). *Jimmy Wales: "I'm Wikipedia's
Monarch"*. Retrieved March 3, 2013, from The Register:
http://www.theregister.co.uk/2013/02/28/jimbo_wales_
wikipedia_monachy/

Why Do You Hate Jimmy Wales. (n.d.). Retrieved March 3, 2013,
from Amplicate: http://amplicate.com/hate/jimmy-wales

Wikimedia . (n.d.). *Wikimedia Statistics.* Retrieved from Wikimedia:
http://stats.wikimedia.org/

Wikimedia Foundation. (n.d.). *Grants.* Retrieved from
Wikimedia.org:
https://meta.wikimedia.org/wiki/Grants:Start

Wikipedia. (n.d.). *Articles to be expanded* . Retrieved from
Wikipedia.org:
https://en.wikipedia.org/wiki/Category:Articles_to_be_e
xpanded

Wikipedia. (n.d.). *Avoid indirect criticism.* Retrieved from
Wikipedia.org:
http://en.wikipedia.org/wiki/Wikipedia:Etiquette#Avoi
d_indirect_criticism

Wikipedia. (n.d.). *Other stuff exists* . Retrieved from Wikipedia.org:
https://en.wikipedia.org/wiki/Wikipedia:Other_stuff_exi
sts

Wikipedia. (n.d.). *Reliable Source Noticeboard.* Retrieved from
Wikipedia.org:
https://en.wikipedia.org/wiki/Wikipedia:Reliable_sourc
es/Noticeboard

Wikipedia. (n.d.). *The Golden Rule*. Retrieved from Wikipedia.org: https://en.wikipedia.org/wiki/Wikipedia:The_answer_to_life,_the_universe,_and_everything

Wikipedia. (n.d.). *Wikipedia Articles for deletion Paul Savramis*. Retrieved from Wikipedia.org: http://en.wikipedia.org/wiki/Wikipedia:Articles_for_deletion/Paul_Savramis

Wikipedia. (n.d.). *Wikipedia:Conflict of interest*. Retrieved from Wikipedia.org: https://en.wikipedia.org/wiki/Wikipedia:Conflict_of_interest

Wood, M. (2013, October 26). *How to Add a Citation in Wikipedia Like an Expert Wikipedia Writer*. Retrieved from Legalmorning.com: http://www.legalmorning.com/how-to-add-a-citation-in-wikipedia-like-an-expert-wikipedia-writer/

Wood, M. (n.d.). *Wikipedia Guide to Notability*. Retrieved from Legalmorning: http://www.legalmorning.com/guide-to-using-wikipedia-for-research/

ABOUT THE AUTHOR

Mike Wood is an online marketer and professional *Wikipedia* editor.

His experience with computers began early in life, when he taught himself how to use a Commodore 64. He gradually moved up through the world of the most up-to-date technology. He recalls being at a Florida swap meet in the 1980's where a vendor was trying to get people to sign up for a new technology called the "Internet." Since then, he has worked in many different professions in the public and private sector. He has used his experience in those industries along with his knowledge of the world of technology to tailor specific online marketing strategies for all of his clients.

Wood runs his own online marketing company Legalmorning.com. Since founding the company, he has helped thousands of people and companies get their articles posted on *Wikipedia*. Hated by *Wikipedia* editors for turning a free website into a money making opportunity, he continues to help those who are shunned by not understanding the thousands of rules and guidelines placed on them by the *Wikipedia* editor hierarchy.

In addition to online marketing services, Wood is the host of the Marketing Impact podcast available on both iTunes and Stitcher. You will also find his work published on sites that include AllBusiness, Business Insider, Huffington Post, Social Media Today, and numerous others.

19916640R00051

Printed in Poland
by Amazon Fulfillment
Poland Sp. z o.o., Wrocław